This journal belongs to

....

I started writing on

this day: ....

in the year: ....

in the city of: ....

and I was .... years old.

I filled up the last page on

this day: ....

in the year: ....

in the city of: ....

when I was .... years old.

It was given to me by:

....

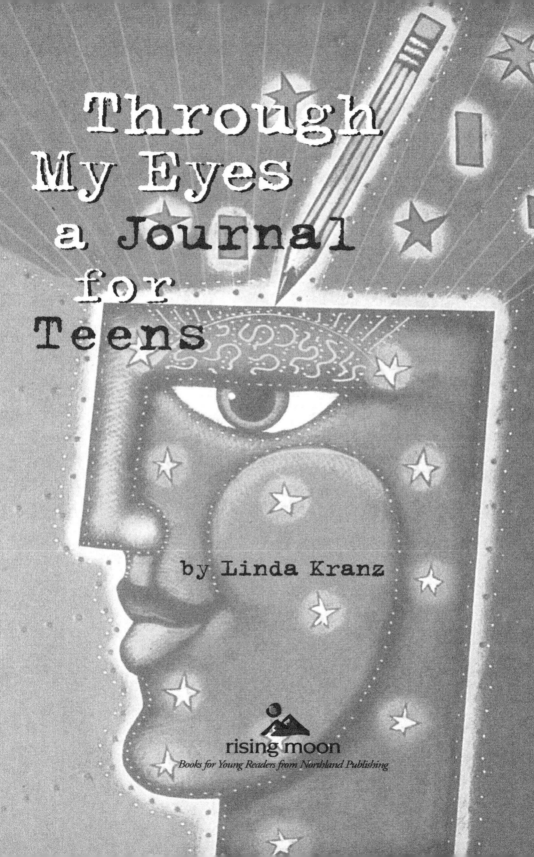

Through My Eyes
a Journal for Teens

by Linda Kranz

rising moon
Books for Young Readers from Northland Publishing

Also by Linda Kranz:

All About Me: A Keepsake Journal for Kids
More About Me: Another Keepsake Journal for Kids
Only One You

These books are available at your local bookstore
or by calling Rising Moon at 1-800-346-3257.

www.risingmoonbooks.com

FIRST IMPRESSION, July 1998
Second Printing, November 1998
Special Books Are Fun, Ltd. Edition, February 1999
ISBN 13: 978-0-87358-715-0
ISBN 10: 0-87358-715-4

For my sister, Kathy, and brothers, Bill, Rory, and Brian. Because of you, I consider myself one of the luckiest big sisters in the world!

And for every teen:

Inside of you there are ideas that can truly make a difference. Share your ideas with the world; make it a better place!

Special Thanks

I would like to thank the people who helped me fine-tune the questions in this journal.

To the following teachers: Mark Bily, who enthusiastically said, "Yes!" when I asked if his students could give me feedback on these questions, and Brian Taylor, Olivia Lorents, and Lynn Fox.

To all the students that took the time to let me know if they would be inspired to answer the questions in this journal. Your responses gave me direction.

Thank you also to Denise Wilson, an English teacher at Hyde Park Middle School in Las Vegas, Nevada, for your suggestions, feedback, and insight.

A big thank you to Suzanne Glazer, from New York City, who tells it like it is! Stephanie Bucholz, Billie Jo Bishop, and *everyone* at Northland Publishing for taking on this journal and making it shine!

To my friends Jann Boylan and Gina Capaldi who have shared their life experiences of raising their teens with me over the years.

Finally, I want to thank my family: Klaus, Jessica, and Nikolaus, for being so understanding about the time I needed to put my thoughts together and get them down on paper. Seeing this journal finished is a dream come true!

A Note about This Journal

A Note About

This Journal...

I have a diary that I kept from my teen years. It was small, and the lines on the pages were narrow. On a two-page spread I was supposed to write a week's worth of memories—hardly enough room to go into detail. When I look at that diary now, I notice that on many days I wrote, "Nothing special happened today. Just an ordinary day." I wish that I had "thought starters" back then; if I had, I know I would have written so much more.

Studies have shown that writing down your thoughts helps you to see things more clearly and to express yourself verbally. Also, you are capturing memories that might otherwise be forgotten. When picture books or chapter books that you have outgrown are given to younger brothers or sisters, or sold or traded to buy new books, your completed journal will be tucked away in a special place, waiting for you to find it again years from now. That is when the true meaning of this journal will come to you: when you pore through its pages, remembering what it was like when you were young.

. . .and a Note about Writing

Look through the questions and find one or two that you want to answer first. You can go in any order. Do the same thing over the next several days. Always date your entries.

At some point, you may decide that you need to take a break from writing for a week or so. That's fine. I suggest leaving your journal in sight. When the time is right you will pick it up again. The most important thing is not to forget about it.

I have included a wide range of topics for you to write about. If you come across a question that you don't have an answer for, just write and answer your own question on that page. There are also several blank pages for you to write or draw whatever you want.

So what are you waiting for? Pick up your pen and start writing! Years from now you will be glad you did!

—Linda Kranz

What are the things that MATTER most to you in your life right now?

....

....

....

....

....

....

....

....

....

....

....

....

....

....

....

....

....

....

....

*Would you always want to
be the same age you are*
RIGHT NOW?
*Why or why not? What
age do you think is the
best age to be?*

If you could change three things about yourself –
appearance, personality, or something else – what would they be and why? How would you go about making these changes?

Name some of the FUNNIEST things that have ever happened to you.

WHEN YOU LOOK IN THE MIRROR, WHAT GOOD THINGS DO YOU SEE?

Remember your first real
CRUSH?
What have you learned
since then? Has anyone
ever broken your heart?
How did you get over it?

Write about some
of your favorite MOVIES.
Write about your favorite
ACTORS. Why do you like them?

Are you open-minded to other people's opinions? Do you listen to all sides before you respond? Are you slow or quick to make a decision? Are you flexible?

Do you usually say what you
         really feel or what you
believe people want to hear?

Why?

DAYDREAM

What do you like to daydream about?

"You don't know how DIFFICULT it was when . . ."

HABITS

Everyone has habits. Write about
a few of yours, good and bad.

Write and answer your own question here.

Ask **WHY?**
    Until you understand.

In order for your **IMAGINATION** to work
        you must use it regularly.

LISTEN to both sides of a story.
    Be **OPEN-MINDED.**

SPECIAL TALENT

Everyone has a special talent; something they do easily or well. What do you do well? Write about how you are developing your talent.

If you could start today over,
what would you do
DIFFERENTLY?

"I'm the **LUCKIEST** person in the world because . . ."

....

....

....

....

....

....

....

....

....

....

....

....

....

....

....

....

....

....

....

....

....

....

....

....

MEMORIES

Write about the memories that come to mind when you think about these phrases: "The laughter of friends," and "Some occasions I won't forget."

If you are having a
BaD dAY,
what cheers you up?
If one of your friends
is feeling DOWN,
how do you help him
or her through it?

Things you wish your parents knew about you . . .

Describe a time when you
felt sorry for someone.

....

....

....

....

....

....

....

....

....

....

....

....

....

....

....

....

....

....

....

....

When you talk to people do you look them in the **eyes?** How do you feel when people speak to you and they don't look directly at you?

Name your
favorite
FOODS and SNACKS.
Write a favorite recipe or two.

What are the latest

clothing and hairstyle

TRENDS?

What are some of

your favorites? Your

least favorites?

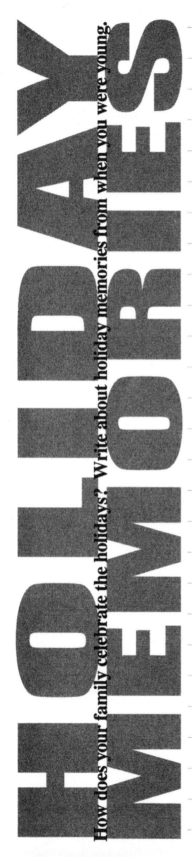

HOLIDAY MEMORIES

How does your family celebrate the holidays? Write about holiday memories from when you were young.

Write or draw anything you want here.

Anything is **POSSIBLE . . .** all you have to do is **TRY.**

Be **UNDERSTANDING.**

Compliment someone today.

What compliments have you received? Who said

COMPL

them, and how did you feel when you heard them?

IMENTS

POSSESSIONS

Name a few of your most prized possessions. Why do they mean so much to you?

"I wanted to write **THIS** down so I wouldn't forget."

It's your

BIRTHDAY !

If you could plan your day, what would you do? When you think back over all the birthdays that you have celebrated, are there a few that stand out in your memory?

_____

_____

_____

_____

_____

_____

_____

_____

_____

_____

_____

_____

_____

_____

_____

_____

_____

What   type
of student are you?
How do you PARTICIPATE
        in class? What are your
STUDY HABITS?

TELEPHONE

It is often said that a telephone is a teenager's best friend.
How do you feel about this statement?

When you are older and have a

place of your own

what will you do that you can't do now?

Every household has

RULES.

Name a few that you

would like to change,

and THE REASONS WHY.

Now that I am

OLDER,

these are the things I have learned about school, about family, about love, about life.

Write about a few of

your most

EMBARRASSING

moments. How did

you get over them?

....

....

....

....

....

....

....

....

....

....

....

....

....

....

....

....

....

....

....

"Some of the things **I WISH FOR** lately more than anything are . . ."

....

....

....

....

....

....

....

....

....

....

....

....

....

....

....

....

....

....

....

....

....

....

....

LOOK AHEAD FIVE YEARS

If you could look ahead five years, what do you think you would see? How do you think your life would be different?

Write and answer your own question here.

BELIEVE in yourself even
when no one else does.

Set aside some quiet
time to **THINK** every day.

Imagine yourself
as a **WINNER** and you will be one.

What is the
HARDEST
thing about growing up?
What is the best thing?
Write about what you
have learned over the
last year. How have
you changed or grown
as a person?

growing and
changing

....

....

....

....

....

....

....

....

....

....

....

....

....

....

....

....

If you could choose to live during any time period, would you live in the future, the past, or right now? Why do you think this would be the best time for you?

SLEEP

Before you drift off to sleep at night, what do you think about?

Are you **involved** in any organizations or clubs? What interested you in them? *If you aren't, are you considering* **joining** one in the near future?

....

....

....

....

....

....

....

....

....

....

....

....

....

....

....

....

....

....

....

....

....

....

....

....

PEER PRESSURE

Write about peer pressure. How often do you notice it and how do you deal with it?

Write about an **event** that you have heard about recently, either on the news, from a family member, or at school, that **affected** you in some way, good or bad.

RELAX

What do you like to do to relax? How do you like to spend your free time?

How would you describe yourself—

appearance and personality

—to someone who doesn't know you?

LOOKING FORWARD

What are you looking forward to tomorrow, this week, this month, and this year?

People are always inventing new products. What would you like to invent that would be important or helpful for people to have in the years to come?

If you could spend a day—morning, afternoon, and night—
being `invisible`, what would you do?

What **time of year** do you like best? Why?

Write about some things that confuse you,
or that you don't understand.

What is your favorite
SMELL, SOUND, COLOR?
Why do you like
them? What do
they remind you of?

ENJOY this time of your life!

TREAT others the way you
want to be **TREATED**

You can be **ANYTHING** you want to be.

Be quick to show your **SMILE**.

Have you ever been

BLAMED

*for something you
didn't do, or has
someone ever taken*

CREDIT

for something you did?

How did you feel?

*How did those things
turn out?*

Do you use a
computer regularly
either at school or at
home? *Do you do
your homework on it,
play games, or keep in
touch with friends by*

e-mail?...

Suppose you are working on a project and no matter what you do, it won't work out right. Would you **keep trying,** take a break and **try again** later, ask for help, or give up?

KEEP TRYING
TRY AGAIN

_____

_____

_____

_____

_____

_____

_____

_____

_____

_____

_____

_____

_____

_____

_____

_____

_____

_____

**Describe your family.
Do you get along with your
brothers and sisters?
Or are you an only child?**

Name ten things that you LOVE. Keep adding to this list.

Do you play
any **SPORTS?**
What do you like
about them?
Or do you prefer
to be the spectator,
cheering
on the team? How do
you give your
support?

Do you offer your HELP around the house? Does Everyone do their part?

Write about some teachers that have made a difference for you and why.

At lunchtime, do you **hang out** *with friends or spend time alone?* Do you pack a lunch or **buy lunch?** *Does your school have an open or closed campus?* Do you stay at school for lunch or leave?

Write and answer your own question here.

LISTEN to different points of view, then do what you think is **RIGHT**.

If you make a **PROMISE**, keep it.

Don't **COMPARE** yourself to others: You are **UNIQUE!**

Do you consider yourself **LUCKY?** *Name some occasions* when luck has favored you. Do you own something that you think is lucky? *Write about why you think it is.*

Which takes more **courage:** telling the **truth** or telling a **lie?** Why do you feel this way?

Have you been

affected by

divorce

either in your own

family or through a

friend? How have

you dealt with those

emotions or helped

a friend deal with

their emotions?

DIVORCE

_____

_____

_____

_____

_____

_____

_____

_____

_____

_____

_____

_____

_____

_____

_____

_____

_____

_____

When you want some QUIET time
alone, to think, where do you go?
Why is it a special place?

"Today started out like any other day, **but then . . .**"

Do you **STAND UP** to people who treat you badly? Write about some things that have happened and how you dealt with them.

Can you tell by looking at someone whether they are friendly or intelligent or if they have the same interests as you? Explain. How long does it take you to get to know someone?

STARGAZE

Have you stargazed into the night sky? What do you think about when you look at the stars?

What do your parents do for a living? Ask your parents what they would choose if they could choose any job. What advice would they give you about deciding on a career?

CAREER JOB LIFESTYLE

CHALLENGE yourself to be
the best you can be.

At the end of the day, think
of three **good things** that
happened to you during the day.
Concentrate on the **positive.**

Keep your head up.
Have **CONFIDENCE** in yourself.

Write about your saddest day and how you made it through that difficult time.

....

....

....

....

....

....

....

....

....

....

....

....

....

....

....

....

....

....

....

....

....

....

_____
_____
_____
_____
_____
_____
_____
_____
_____
_____
_____
_____
_____
_____
_____
_____
_____
_____
_____
_____
_____
_____
_____
_____
_____

What type of music do you like?
Name some of your favorite songs and musicians.

MUSIC

Write down some of your favorite lyrics.
How does listening to your favorite music make you feel?

LYRICS

Words are changing all the
time, and people are always
making up new phrases.
Write down a few of the
popular expressions or words
you and your friends use
and include their meanings.

cool
dude

CAREERS?
SCHOOL?
BUSINESS?

What career or careers have you been thinking about? Why do these jobs appeal to you? Are you planning to go to college or a trade school or will you go right into the work force? *What steps are you taking to prepare?*

What is your outlook
on life? Do you
consider yourself an

OPTIMIST

or a

PESSIMIST?

Why do you
feel this way?

Why do you think **friends** enjoy being with you? What makes your friends feel **comfortable** about being around you?

Write about your best **qualities** and **strengths**.

How do you feel about getting your driver's license? At what age do you think teens should be able to drive? *If you already have your license, what was it like getting*

behind the wheel

for the first time? What have you learned since you started driving?

If your parents were
gone for a **month**
or so and you were
on your own, how
would you **spend**
your days?

Write and answer your own question here.

Be **ENTHUSIASTIC!**

Practice the skill of **LISTENING**.
Really **HEAR** what others are saying.

In your own special way, show
your loved ones, the most important
people in your life, that you love them.
Tell them often that you love them.
REACH OUT!

Are you a **good listener?**
Do you let people finish
their sentences, or do you
jump in and start **talking?**

Write about things **your parents have done** that surprised you.

....

....

....

....

....

....

....

....

....

....

....

....

....

....

....

....

....

....

....

....

....

....

....

REFLECTIVE

Do you consider yourself to be outgoing or quiet and reflective?

Do you see your relatives —aunts, uncles, grandparents—often? If so, write about memories from your visits. If not, how do you stay in touch?

Cousins, grandparents...

PROBLEM

What do you think are the three main problems in the world right now? Do you see the solution to them? If it was up to you, how would you change the world?

SOLUTION

What makes you **HAPPY?**

Make a list of things you want to accomplish

ACCOMPL

during your lifetime. Keep adding to the list.

ISHMENTS

Dream **BIG!** Stay **FOCUSED!**

In this world you **GET** what you **GIVE**. Always give your **BEST!**

Be patient. Through **EXPERIENCE**, so many things become clearer.

If you could pick out **any car,** what would you choose?

....

....

....

....

....

....

....

....

....

....

....

....

....

....

....

....

....

....

....

....

MAILBOX

If you opened your mailbox and inside there was a check made out to you for one million dollars, how would you use the money?

Is there someone you know whom you can trust to tell your **innermost thoughts?** Someone that won't spread them around? Who is this person?

_____

_____

_____

_____

_____

_____

_____

_____

_____

_____

_____

_____

_____

_____

_____

_____

_____

Do you have a pet? If so, what do you like most or least about him or her? If not, what would your **perfect** pet be?

What are your FEARS?
Is there someone you can discuss
them with?

_____

_____

_____

_____

_____

_____

_____

_____

_____

_____

_____

_____

_____

_____

_____

_____

If you could

TRAVEL

anywhere in the

world, where would

you go and why?

Have you ever lost someone close to you?
Write about your feelings and
memories. Why was this person
special to you?

YEAR 2050

What do you think the world will be like in the year 2050?

Is there someone you know whose smile makes you
FEEL GOOD? Who is it?

How did you meet? How long

have you known each other?

_____

_____

_____

_____

_____

_____

_____

_____

_____

_____

_____

_____

_____

Follower or LEADER

Do you consider yourself a trendsetter or trendspotter, a leader or a follower? Why do you feel this way?

What is
the most meaningful
and important HUG
you ever remember?

**What feelings come to mind when you
think about that hug?**

~~~~~~
~~~~~~
~~~~~~
~~~~~~
~~~~~~
~~~~~~
~~~~~~
~~~~~~
~~~~~~
~~~~~~
~~~~~~
~~~~~~
~~~~~~
~~~~~~
~~~~~~
~~~~~~
~~~~~~
~~~~~~
~~~~~~
~~~~~~
~~~~~~
~~~~~~
~~~~~~
~~~~~~
~~~~~~

What have you learned

about being a

FRIEND?

Describe some of your

friends: How do you

complement each other?

IF you could own

your own BUSINESS

what would it be?

How do you convince your parents to let you **try** *something that you have never done before? Describe a few occasions when you were allowed to do something for the* **first time.** *What were they and how did you feel?*

....

....

....

....

....

....

....

....

....

....

....

....

....

....

....

....

....

....

....

Have you ever given **your word** *to someone but then didn't follow through? How do you regain a person's* **trust** *when you have let that person down?*

Do you take suggestions easily
or do you get **defensive?**
How do you react?

_____

_____

_____

_____

_____

_____

_____

_____

_____

_____

_____

_____

_____

_____

_____

_____

_____

_____

_____

_____

_____

_____

What is your favorite book? Why do you like it? Name a few of your other favorite books.

Think back over the years
    and write about some things your
parents have taught you that you will
        always carry with you.

_____

_____

_____

_____

_____

_____

_____

_____

_____

_____

_____

_____

_____

_____

_____

_____

_____

_____

Write down the cost of a first-class stamp, a gallon of gas, a ticket to the movies, *a CD,* a candy bar, *and a few other items.* It will be interesting to look back and see how prices have changed years from now.

$$$

Describe your

BEDROOM.

Do you share or have

it all to yourself?

What do you like or

dislike about your

room? *If you could*

redesign your room,

where would you start?

Write about something that you **enjoy doing.** How did you get interested in it? Why do you **like it** so much?

....

....

....

....

....

....

....

....

....

....

....

....

....

....

....

....

....

....

....

....

....

....

ADMIRABLE QUALITIES

Write about someone you look up to: a friend, a relative, or a famous person. What qualities do you admire in this person? Name a few others you admire.

How do you

feel about your

generation?

Write about some of

the challenges you

and other teens

are facing today.

VACATION

Where would you like to go on vacation this year? Why do you want to go there?

....
....
....
....
....
....
....
....
....
....
....
....
....
....
....
....
....
....
....
....
....
....
....

Make a list of things you are THANKFUL for.

About the Author

Linda Kranz began writing as a teenager. A locking diary given to her for her thirteenth birthday was the vehicle that encouraged her to take to the page. Growing up in a military family and moving around often gave her plenty to write about. But it was her daughter's interest in keeping a journal of her own that inspired Linda to write her first book, *All About Me: A Keepsake Journal for Kids*, which lead to *More About Me: Another Keepsake Journal For Kids*, also from Northland Publishing. Linda and her husband, Klaus, live with their children, Jessica and Nikolaus, in the mountains of Flagstaff, Arizona.

The author would enjoy hearing from you about your thoughts on journal writing and any suggestions you may have for future journals. Write her at:

Linda Kranz
c/o Rising Moon
P.O. Box 1389
Flagstaff, Az 86002–1389